CHRISTMAS

Arranged for Easy Piano by Carol Tornquist

Now you can play the music from church that you love to hear and sing with the *Pure & Simple* series. Each book features lyrics, suggested fingerings, phrasing, pedal markings, and easy-to-read notation. The solo piano arrangements, which use familiar harmonies and rhythms, will put your favorite melodies at your fingertips quickly and easily.

This volume features Christmas carols, which are an essential part of the holiday season. Carols are a continuous source of joy and have been sung for centuries. Their lyrics, whether uplifting or peaceful, are perfect for personal moments of reflection as well as for sing-along gatherings and celebrations with loved ones. Additionally, carols are a staple in any pianist's repertoire.

D1441121

Alfred Music Publishing Co., Inc.
P.O. Box 10003
Van Nuys, CA 91410-0003
alfred.com

ISBN-10: 0-7390-9170-0
ISBN-13: 978-0-7390-9170-8

Cover Photo
Christmas wreath 1: © iStockphoto.com / mikehome

CONTENTS

ANGELS WE HAVE HEARD ON HIGH

Traditional French carol
Arranged by Carol Tornquist

Brightly

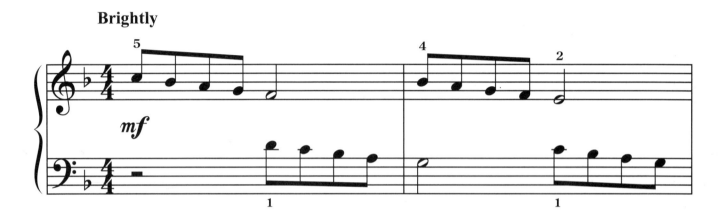

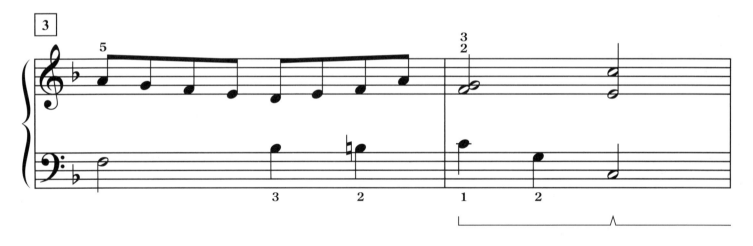

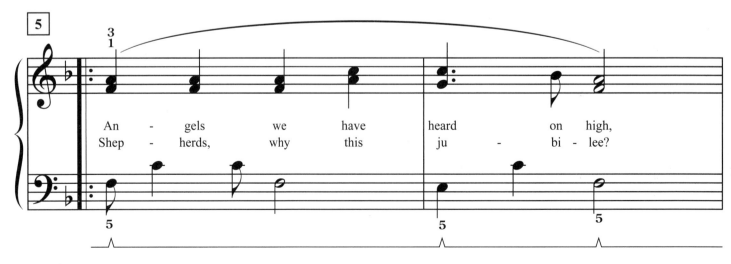

An - gels   we   have   heard   on   high,
Shep - herds,   why   this   ju - bi - lee?

Away in a Manger

Music by James R. Murray
Arranged by Carol Tornquist

Slowly and gently

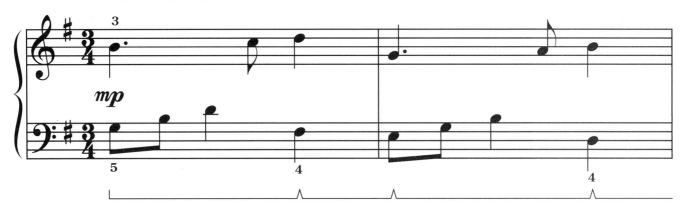

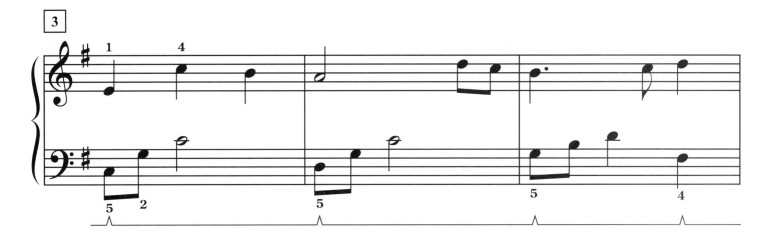

DECK THE HALL

Welsh carol
Arranged by Carol Tornquist

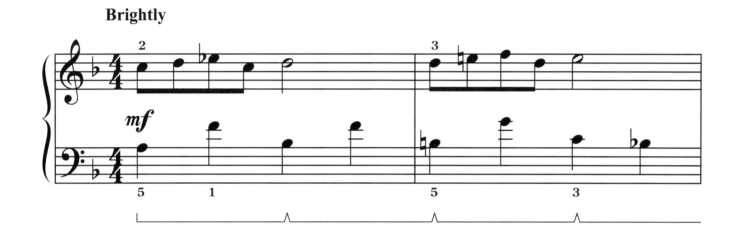

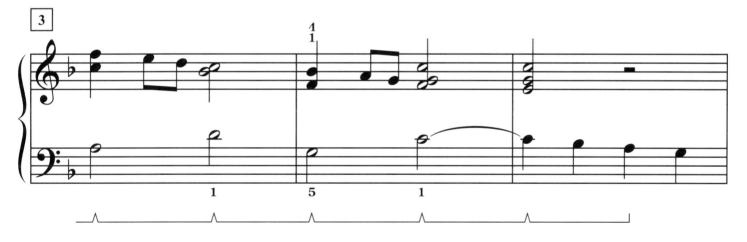

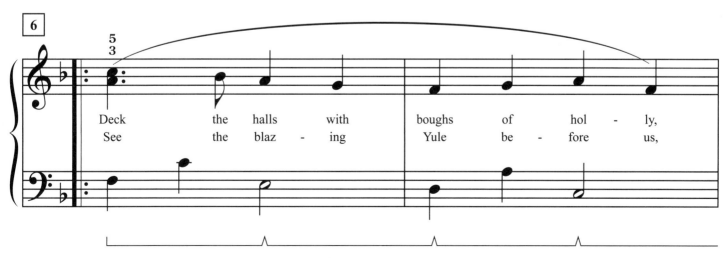

Deck   the halls   with   boughs   of   hol - ly,
See   the   blaz - ing   Yule   be - fore   us,

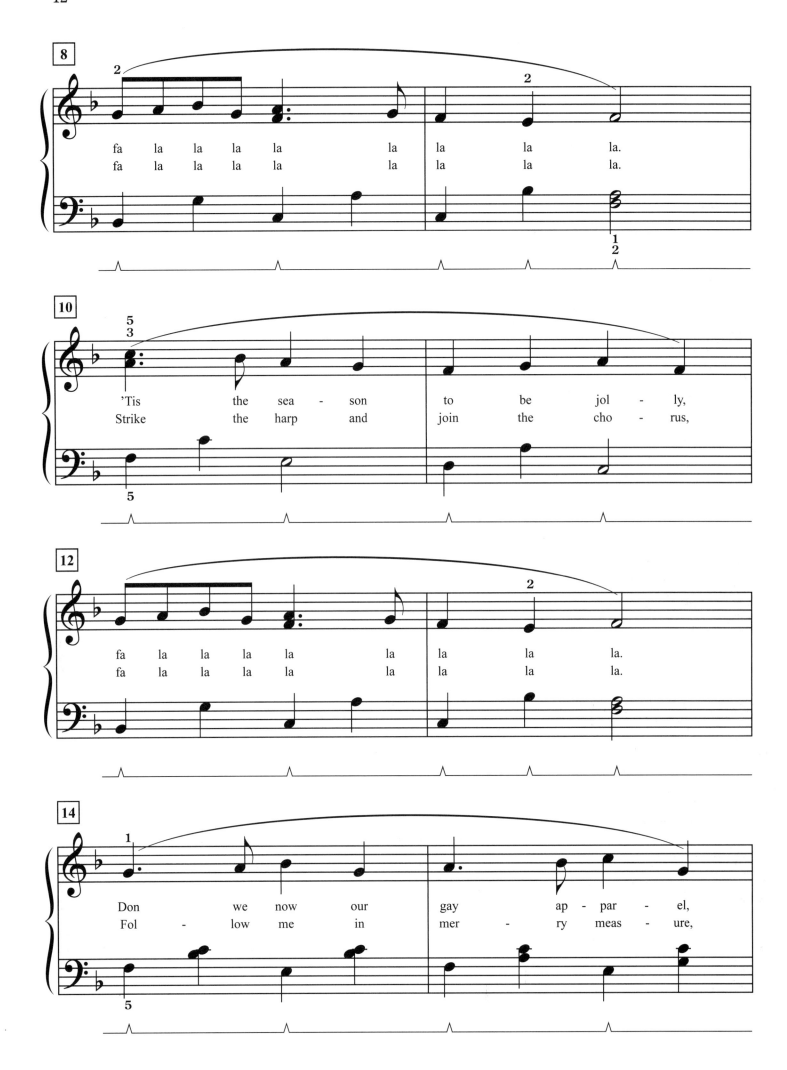

COVENTRY CAROL

Traditional English carol
Arranged by Carol Tornquist

Moderately slow

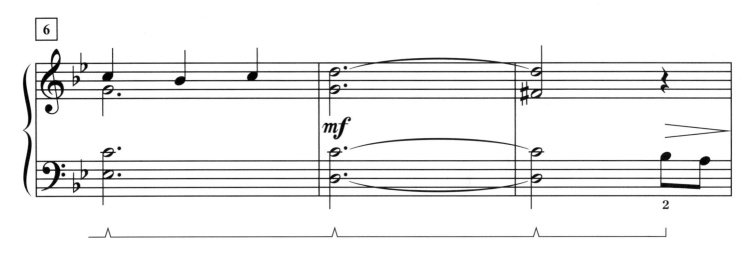

16

THE FIRST NOEL

Traditional English carol
Arranged by Carol Tornquist

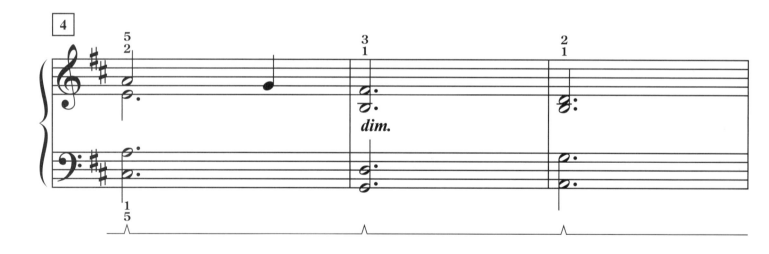

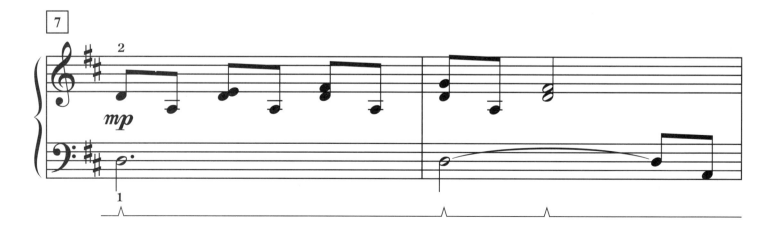

Go, Tell It on the Mountain

Words by John W. Work, Jr.
Spiritual
Arranged by Carol Tornquist

24

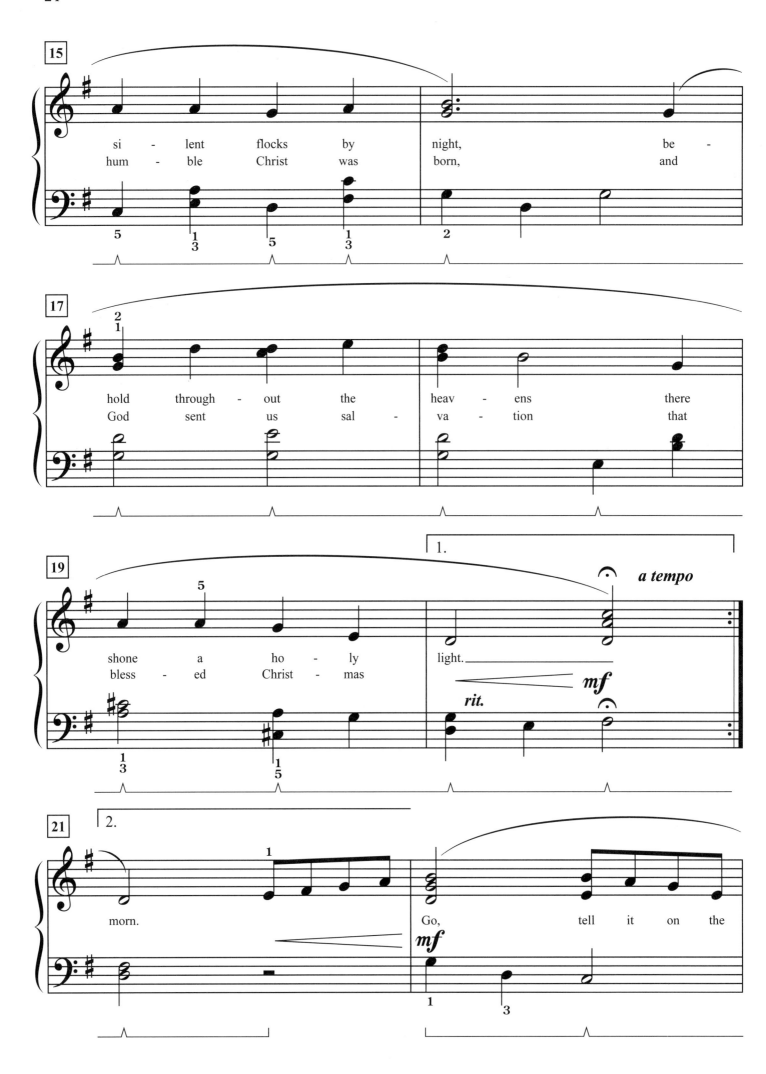

25

Hark! the Herald Angels Sing

Words by Charles Wesley
Music by Felix Menelssohn
Arranged by Carol Tornquist

Joyously

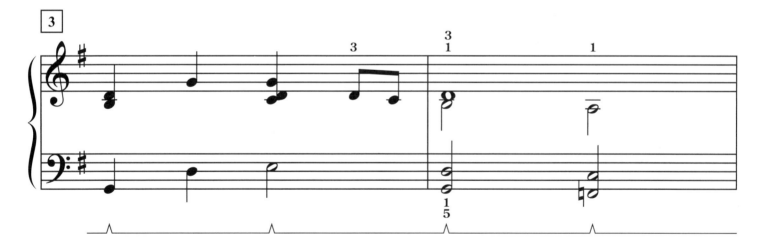

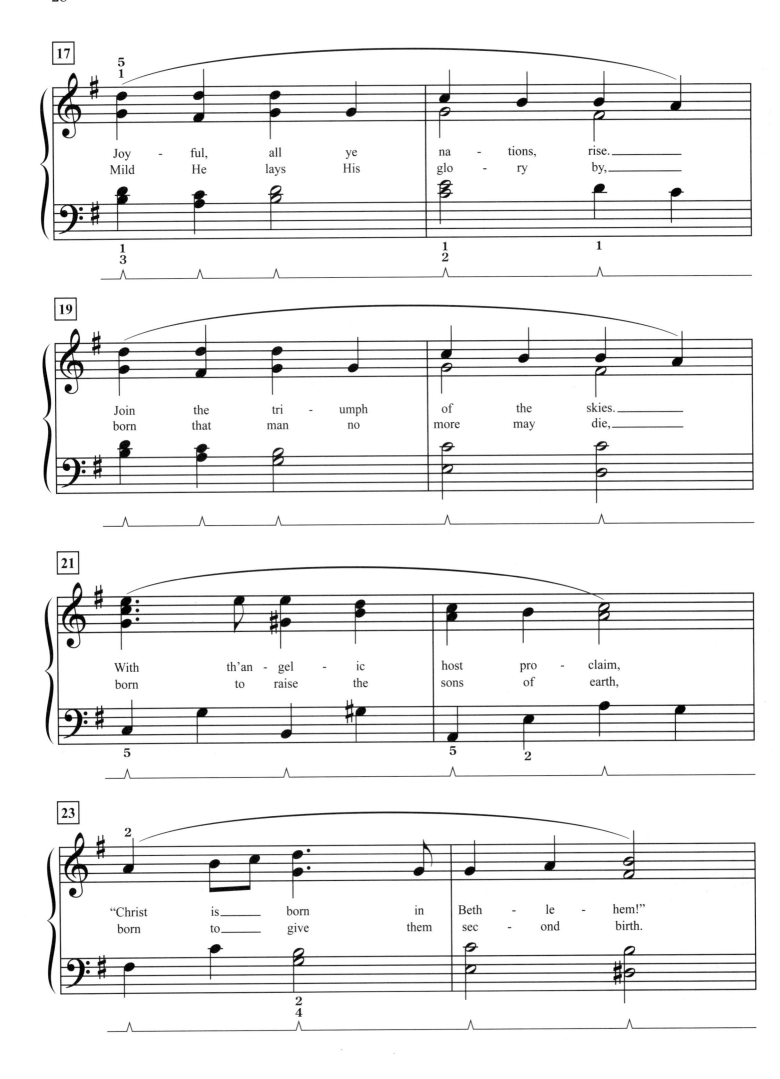

29

Infant Holy, Infant Lowly

Traditional Polish carol
Arranged by Carol Tornquist

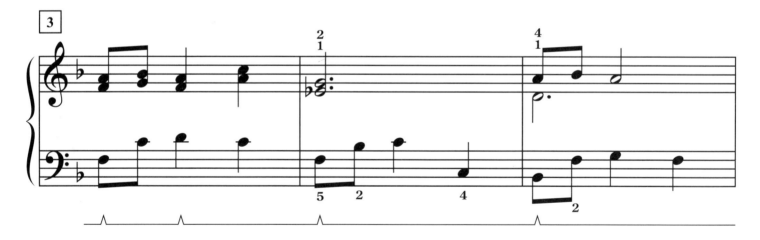

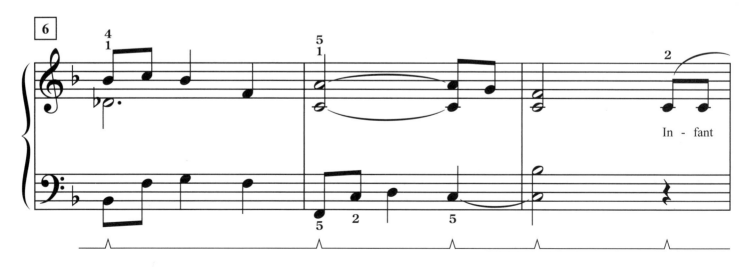

It Came upon the Midnight Clear

Words by Edmund H. Sears
Music by Richard S. Willis
Arranged by Carol Tornquist

Peacefully

It
lo!

came
the

up - on
days

the
are

JOY TO THE WORLD

Words by Isaac Watts
Music by Lowell Mason
Arranged by Carol Tornquist

Joyfully

O LITTLE TOWN OF BETHLEHEM

Words by Phillips Brooks
Music by Lewis H. Redner
Arranged by Carol Tornquist

Tenderly

40

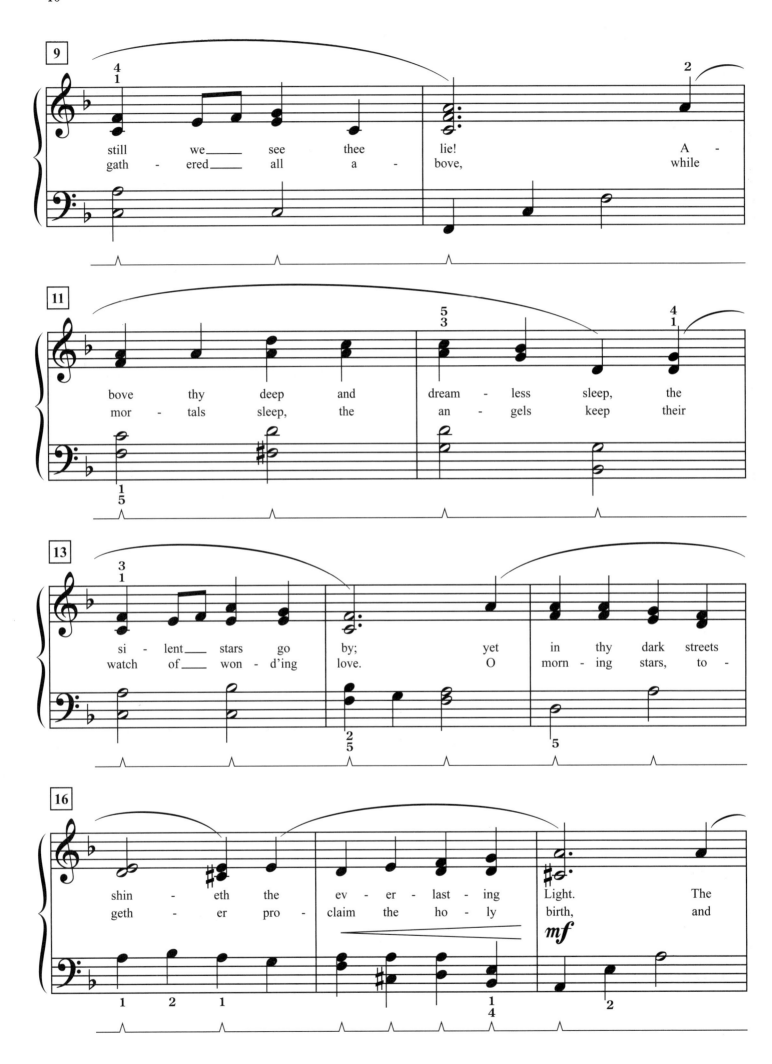

O CHRISTMAS TREE
(O Tannenbaum)

Traditional German carol
Arranged by Carol Tornquist

Moderately

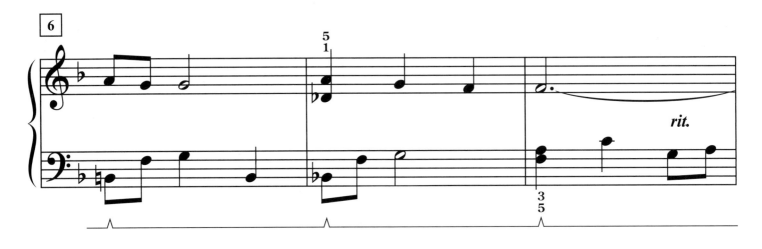

44

O Come, All Ye Faithful

Latin hymn
Music by John Francis Wade
Arranged by Carol Tornquist

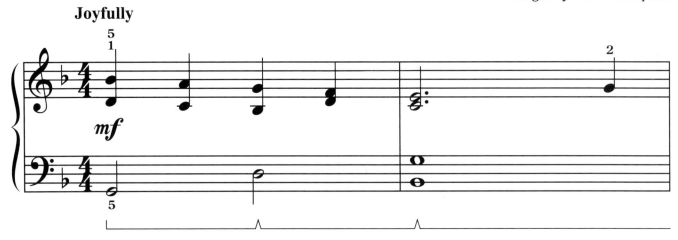

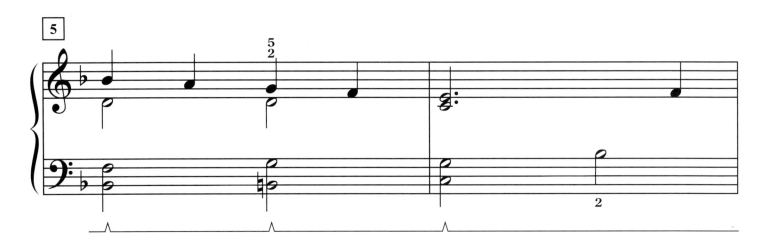

48

O Come, O Come, Emmanuel

Latin hymn
Plainsong: adapt. Thomas Helmore
Arranged by Carol Tornquist

Moderately slow

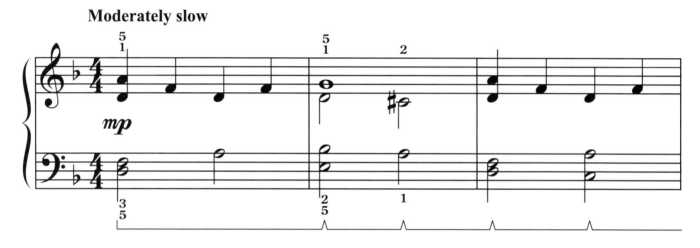

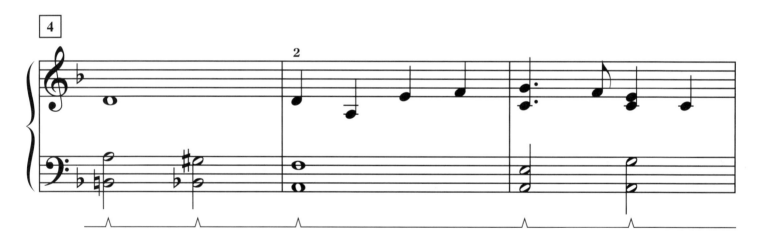

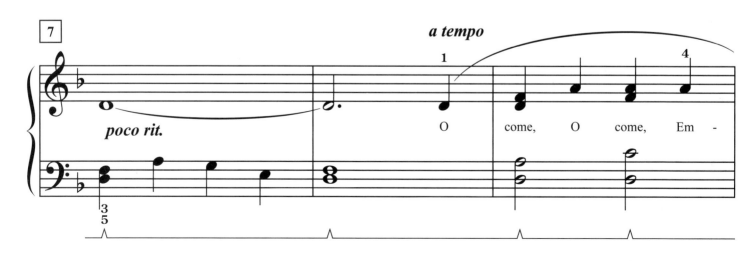

O come, O come, Em -

52

el   shall come to thee,   O   Is -   ra -

el!

SING WE NOW OF CHRISTMAS

Traditional French carol
Arranged by Carol Tornquist

Moderately, in two

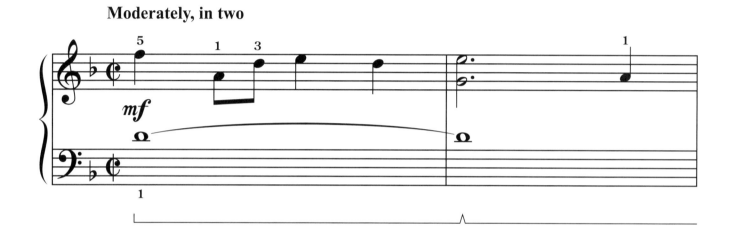

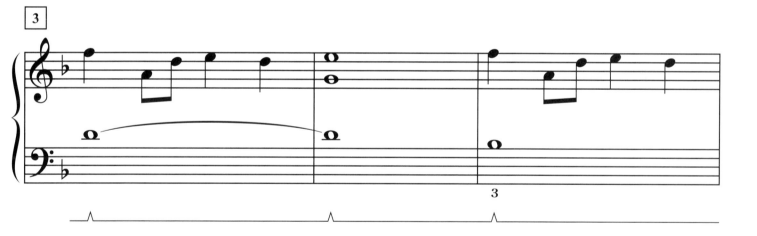

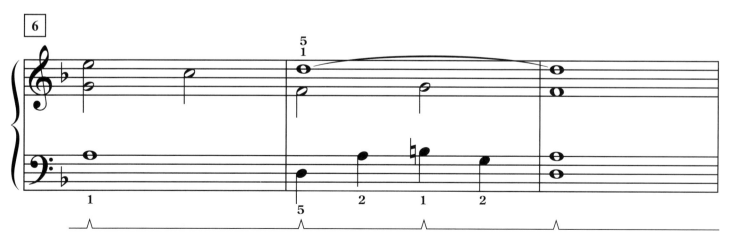

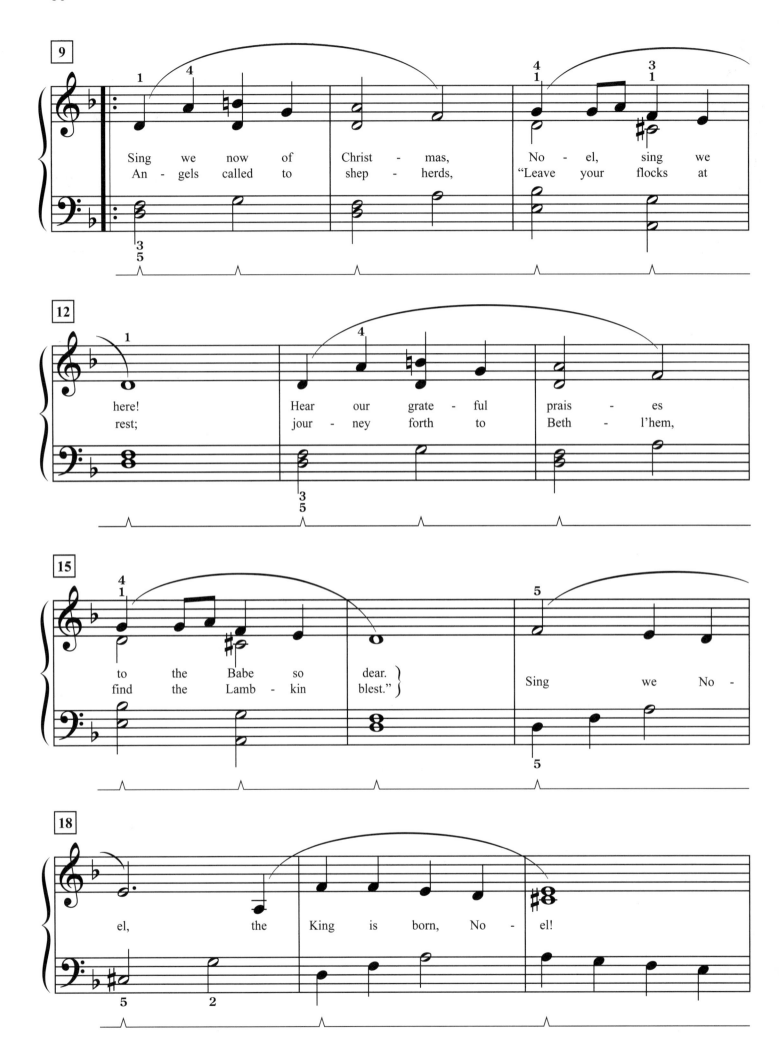

Sing we now of Christ - mas, sing we___ now No -

el!

cresc.

f

SILENT NIGHT

Words by Joseph Mohr
Music by Franz Grüber
Arranged by Carol Tornquist

Slowly and tenderly

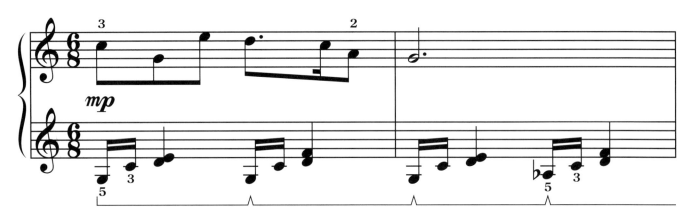

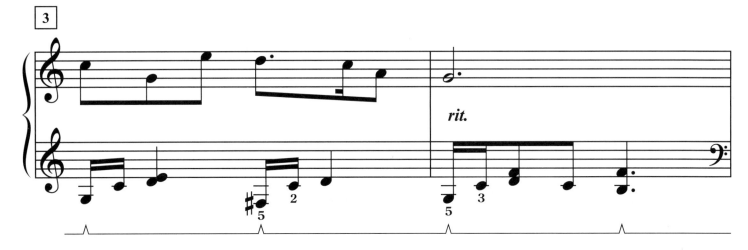

Si - lent night, ho - ly night,
Si - lent night, ho - ly night,

60

Still, Still, Still

Traditional Austrian carol
Arranged by Carol Tornquist

Moderately slow, hushed

Ukrainian Bell Carol

Mykola Leontovych
Arranged by Carol Tornquist

Lively

WE THREE KINGS OF ORIENT ARE

Words and Music by
John Henry Hopkins, Jr.
Arranged by Carol Tornquist

Moderately slow

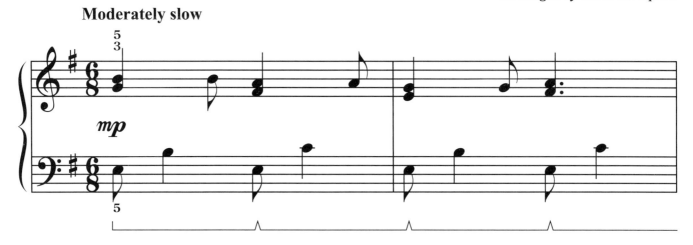

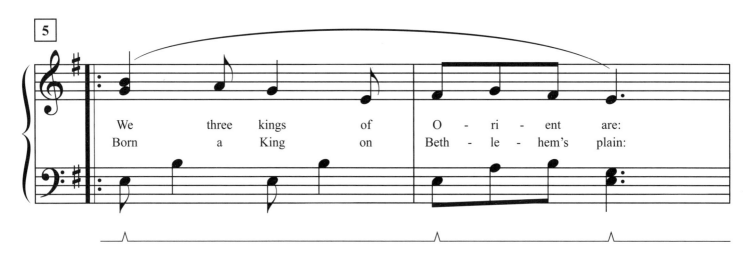

We three kings of O – ri – ent are:
Born a King on Beth – le – hem's plain:

72

WHAT CHILD IS THIS?

Words by William Chatterton Dix
Traditional English melody
Arranged by Carol Tornquist

74

WE WISH YOU A MERRY CHRISTMAS

Traditional English carol
Arranged by Carol Tornquist

Brightly

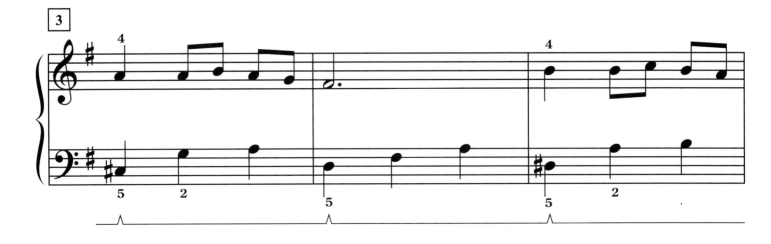

77

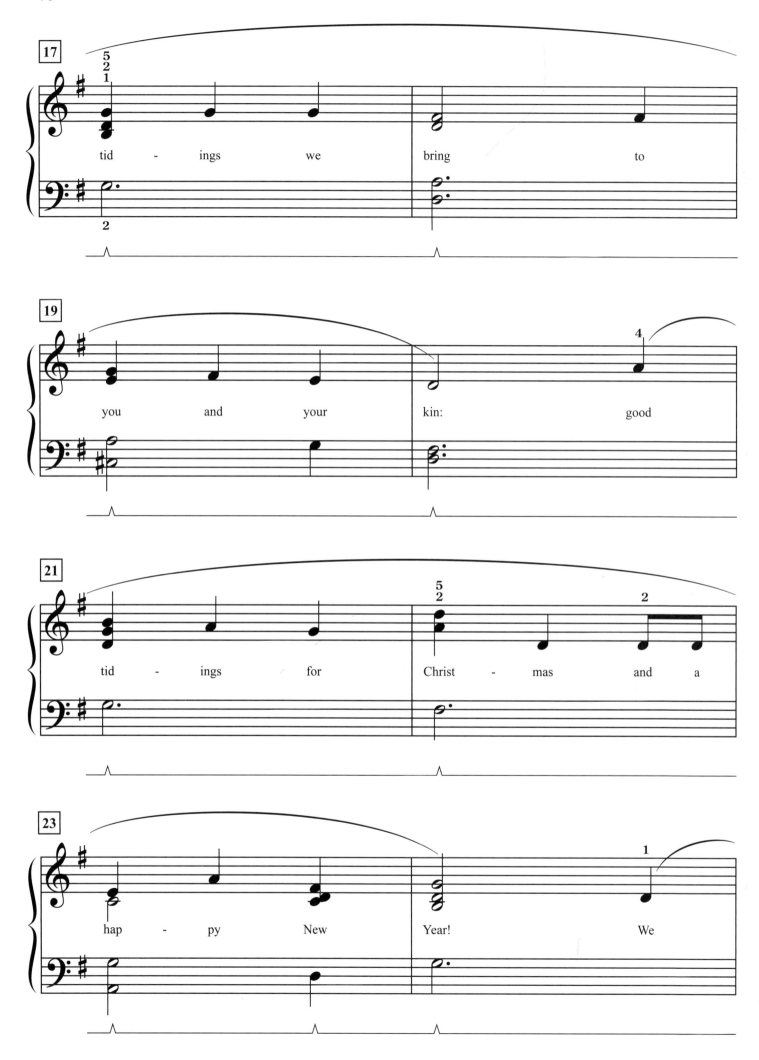